This book belongs to:

....

To: Gabe & Maddie
With Love,
From: Mimi & Baba
Christmas 2017

....

On:

....

© 2015 by Barbour Publishing, Inc.

Print ISBN 978-1-63409-032-2

eBook Editions:
Adobe Digital Edition (.epub) 978-1-63409-585-3
Kindle and MobiPocket Edition (.prc) 978-1-63409-586-0

All scripture quotations are taken from the King James Version of the Bible.

Cover and interior illustrations: David Miles Illustration, www.davidmiles.us

Published by Barbour Books, an imprint of Barbour Publishing, Inc., P.O. Box 719, Uhrichsville, Ohio 44683, www.barbourbooks.com

Our mission is to publish and distribute inspirational products offering exceptional value and biblical encouragement to the masses.

ecpa Member of the
Evangelical Christian
Publishers Association

Printed in China.
05116 0815 IM

Christmas Prayers & Stories for Bedtime

JEAN FISCHER ✳ RENAE BRUMBAUGH

ILLUSTRATED BY **DAVID MILES**

BARBOUR BOOKS
An Imprint of Barbour Publishing, Inc.

KIDS LOVE CHRISTMAS!

Jesus' birthday is the perfect time to celebrate family togetherness, and here are more than 60 carefully retold Bible stories and prayers surrounding the birth of our Savior—from God's Old Testament promise of a king to the baby's manger bed and the angels' visit to the shepherds. Each story is paired with a memorable passage of scripture, and takes your kids beyond the story itself. They'll be challenged to consider how these Christmas stories relate to their lives today. Packed with colorful illustrations and thoughtful prayer starters, *Christmas Prayers & Stories for Bedtime* is the perfect book to bring you and your kids together for some spiritual quality time this holiday season. Enjoy!

God's Promise

*Therefore the Lord
himself shall give you a sign;
Behold, a virgin shall conceive,
and bear a son, and shall
call his name Immanuel.*

Isaiah 7:14

Long before anyone had ever heard about Jesus, God made a promise. "I will send someone to save the world," He said. The world needed saving because its people did things that made God unhappy. But those people belonged to God! They were His children. He did not want to punish them for the bad things they did. So God made a plan to send His Son, Jesus, to save the world.

God's plan was perfect. He planned to send Jesus into the world as a baby. And when Jesus grew up, He would teach the people how God wanted them to live. Jesus would love the people so much that He would take all the punishment that they deserved—forever!

God's promise came with an extra-special surprise. Everyone who believed in Jesus would get to live in heaven one day with Jesus and God. And the best part is that God's promise was not just for those people long ago. His promise is for you!

Dear Father,
it makes me happy
that You love me.
Thank You for always
keeping Your promises.
Help me to keep
my promises, too.

HERE WE COME A-CAROLING

Here we come a-caroling
Among the leaves so green,
Here we come a-wand'ring,
So fair to be seen.

Chorus:

Love and joy come to you,

And to your carol too,

And God bless you and send

you a happy New Year,

And God send you a

happy New Year.

TRADITIONAL ENGLISH CAROL

Frightened!

And the angel said unto her,
*Fear not, Mary: for thou hast
found favour with God. And, behold,
thou shalt conceive in thy womb,
and bring forth a son,
and shalt call his name* JESUS.

LUKE 1:30–31

One night, a young girl named Mary was sleeping. Suddenly, a loud voice woke her up! She opened her eyes to a bright light, and she didn't know what was happening. Mary covered her face, wanting to hide from whatever was in her room. But peeking through her fingers, she saw a beautiful creature all in white.

"Greetings, Mary!" said the angel, whose name was Gabriel. "Don't be afraid. God thinks you are really special. He wants you to be the mother of His Son. You will name Him, 'Jesus.'"

Mary was afraid, and didn't know what to think. She had never seen an angel before. Maybe she wanted to cry, or tell the angel to go away. Maybe she wanted to run away herself! But she didn't. She loved God, and she was willing to do whatever God wanted her to do.

God had a plan to bless Mary, and He wanted to bless the whole world through her. Even though she was frightened, she chose to obey God.

Dear Father, I thank You for sending Jesus. I'm glad Mary obeyed You, even though she was afraid. When I feel afraid, help me to remember that You love me and that I am special to You.

THE ANGEL GABRIEL FROM HEAVEN CAME

The angel Gabriel from
Heaven came,
His wings as drifted snow,
his eyes as flame;
"All hail," said he, "thou
lowly maiden Mary,
Most highly favored lady,"
Gloria!

"For know a blessèd
mother thou shalt be,
All generations laud
and honor thee,
Thy Son shall be Emmanuel,
by seers foretold,
Most highly favored lady,"
Gloria!

BASQUE CAROL
TRANSLATED BY SABINE BARING-GOULD

Patience

Wait on the Lord: *be of good courage,*
and he shall strengthen thine heart:
wait, I say, on the Lord.
Psalm 27:14

Has anyone ever told you to be patient? Has anyone ever told you to wait?

Patience is what God expected from His people. He expected them to wait for what He had promised them. The people wanted Jesus to come right away to save the world. But God decided they should wait.

Waiting was hard. It was like knowing they were getting a really special present for Christmas and they had to wait until Christmas morning to open it. But while the people waited, God gave them little hints. He told them a tiny bit about Jesus' mother. He told them Jesus' name and even some of His nicknames, like Immanuel and Prince of Peace. He said that Baby Jesus would be born in a little town called Bethlehem. But God did not say *when* Jesus would come. He decided, "You will just have to wait."

So, the people waited. . .and they waited. . .and they waited. They waited for days and months, and then they waited for years! As best they could, God's people waited patiently.

Dear Father, waiting is hard for me sometimes. I try my best to be patient, but it doesn't always work. So, please give me the patience I need!

Little Children, Wake and Listen

Little children, wake and listen!
Songs are breaking o'er the earth;
While the stars in heaven glisten,
Hear the news of Jesus' birth.

Long ago, to lovely meadows,
Angels brought the message down;
Still, each year, through
midnight shadows,
It is heard in every town.

UNKNOWN

The King

He shall be great, and shall be called the Son of the Highest: and the Lord God shall give unto him the throne of his father David: And he shall reign over the house of Jacob for ever; and of his kingdom there shall be no end.

LUKE 1:32–33

Most kings inherit their crowns from their fathers. When a king is born, he is called a prince. Then, when he is old enough, he becomes the king, and he rules over his kingdom. When he dies, or perhaps when he is too old to be a good ruler, one of his sons will become the king.

Sometimes, a king will lose his kingdom altogether. Perhaps there is a war, and another country steals his kingdom away. Or perhaps the people of his own kingdom decide they want a different king.

Jesus is a different kind of king, for His kingdom will never end. He is called the Prince of Peace, but He is also the King of Kings. He has always been the king, and He always will be.

He is a good and kind ruler. He will never die, so He will never have to pass His crown on to anyone else. And no matter who may try to take His kingdom from Him, they will never win. The kingdom of God will remain forever, and Jesus will always be its ruler.

Dear Father, thank You for sending Jesus to be a good and kind ruler. I'm glad He is the king, and that His kingdom will last forever.

THERE'S A SONG IN THE AIR

There's a song in the air!
There's a star in the sky!
There's a mother's deep prayer
And a baby's low cry!
And the star rains its fire
While the beautiful sing,
For the manger of Bethlehem
Cradles a King!

There's a tumult of joy
O'er the wonderful birth,
For the virgin's sweet boy
Is the Lord of the earth.
Ay! the star rains its fire
While the beautiful sing,
For the manger of Bethlehem
Cradles a King!

JOSIAH HOLLAND

Trust

Some trust in chariots, and some
in horses: but we will remember
the name of the Lord *our God.*

Psalm 20:7

While they waited, God expected His people to trust Him to do exactly what He had promised. Trust means believing in someone or something with all of your heart. God wanted His people to believe with all of their hearts that He would send Jesus to save the world. But some people found it hard to trust God because they could not see Him. They trusted only in things that they *could* see, like chariots (chariots were carts that soldiers rode in) and the horses that pulled them. This made God sad.

A good plan takes time. Those who trusted God believed that His plan was good, and they understood they had to wait while God put His plan together. They believed in God's goodness, and they knew that God loved them. With all of their hearts, they believed that God's plan would work out perfectly. So those people trusted God, and they looked forward to Jesus coming to save the world.

You should trust God, too. Do you know why? Because God has a plan for you, and His plan is very good.

Dear Father, thank You for having a good plan for me. I believe that You love me, and I trust You to take care of me.

THE TRUTH SENT FROM ABOVE

This is the truth sent from above,
The truth of God, the God of love;
Therefore don't turn me from your door,
But hearken all, both rich and poor.

And at this season of the year
Our blest Redeemer did appear
He here did live, and here did preach,
And many thousands He did teach.

TRADITIONAL ENGLISH FOLK CAROL

Adopted

*Now the birth of Jesus Christ was on
this wise: When as his mother Mary was
espoused to Joseph, before they came
together, she was found with
child of the Holy Ghost.*

MATTHEW 1:18

Mary and Joseph were planning to get married. They were excited about the wedding. They probably had a big celebration planned, with many guests and a delicious feast. Like most couples, they looked forward to having children some day.

But then Mary and Joseph learned that their first child would be God's Son! They would be parents sooner than they expected.

Jesus had two fathers. Joseph was His adopted father. Joseph loved Jesus, and he taught Jesus all the things that a good father teaches his son. Joseph taught Him how to be a carpenter and how to be a good man. But God was Jesus' father, too. It was important for everyone to know that Jesus was truly God's son. God sent Him as a gift to the world.

Just as Joseph adopted Jesus and raised Him as his own son, God wants to adopt each of us to be His children. He loves us, and He will teach us the things we need to know in life.

Dear Father, thank You for sending Your very own Son as a gift to the world. Just as Joseph adopted Jesus, I know You want to adopt me and make me Your own child. Thank You for loving me and teaching me how to live.

Ye Sons of Men, Oh, Hearken

Ye sons of men, oh, hearken:
Your heart and mind prepare;
To hail th'almighty Savior,
Oh sinners, be your care.
He who of grace alone
Our Life and Light was given,
The promised Lord from Heaven,
Unto our world is shown.

Prepare my heart, Lord Jesus,
Turn not from me aside,
And grant that I receive Thee
This blessèd Adventide.
From stall and manger low
Come Thou to dwell within me;
Loud praises will I sing Thee
And forth Thy glory show.

VALENTIN THILO
TRANSLATED BY ARTHUR RUSSELL

A Perfect Plan

*For I know the thoughts that I think
toward you, saith the L{ORD},
thoughts of peace, and not of evil,
to give you an expected end.*

JEREMIAH 29:11

What seemed like a long time to God's people was just like a blink of an eye to God. His time, heaven time, is not like time here on earth. God knew exactly how He would work out His plan to send Jesus to save the world. And God knew all about Jesus long before He arrived here as a baby. After all, Jesus had been God's Son forever. He will always be God's Son.

Do you know that you are a child of God, too? You are! God made you. God knows everything about you. He knew you before you were born. He had a perfect plan to send you into the world, and He has your whole life planned out. Much of it is a secret. You will find out more about God's plan as you grow up. But His plan for you is like His plan for Jesus—perfect in every way. Part of God's plan is this: He will be your heavenly Father forever.

Dear Father, thank You for making me and for knowing all about me. I can't wait to see the wonderful plan You have for my life!

O COME, LITTLE CHILDREN

O come, little children,
from near and afar,
And gaze on the wonder
'neath Bethlehem's star.
God sent His own Son
as a dear little boy
To be your redeemer,
your hope, and your joy.

Come, kneel and adore Him
like shepherds today,
Lift up little hands now
and praise Him as they.
Rejoice that the Savior was
sent you this night,
And join in the song of
the angels of light.

CHRISTOPH VON SCHMID

New Dad

*But while he thought on these things, behold, the angel of the L*ORD *appeared unto him in a dream, saying, Joseph, thou son of David, fear not to take unto thee Mary thy wife: for that which is conceived in her is of the Holy Ghost. And she shall bring forth a son, and thou shalt call his name J*ESUS*: for he shall save his people from their sins.*

MATTHEW 1:20–21

Joseph was surprised to learn that Mary was going to have a baby. At first, he wasn't sure if he wanted to adopt her son or not. One night, while he was trying to figure out what to do, he had a dream.

In this dream, an angel spoke to him. The angel said, "Joseph, don't be afraid to make Mary your wife and adopt her son. He is God's Son, but He will need a dad here on earth. His name will be Jesus, and He will be a blessing to the whole world."

Joseph obeyed God and adopted Jesus. He became Jesus' dad, and he was proud of his son. Sometimes, when we're not sure what to do, we can just wait. If we ask God to help us, He will show us what He wants us to do.

Dear Father, sometimes I don't know what to do. Help me to always look to You for answers. I know that You will help me to do the right thing. Thank You for leading me in the way I should go.

Joseph Dearest, Joseph Mine or Song of the Crib

"Joseph, Dearest Joseph mine,
Help me cradle the Child divine.
God reward thee and all that's thine,
In paradise," so prays the mother Mary.

He came among us at Christmas time
At Christmas time in Bethlehem
Men shall bring him from far and wide,
Love's diadem Jesus, Jesus;
Lo, he comes and loves and
saves and frees us.

Gladly dear one, Lady mine
Help I cradle this Child of thine."
"God's own light on us both shall shine,
In paradise," as prays the mother Mary.

TRADITIONAL GERMAN CAROL, 14TH CENTURY

Forgotten?

*But the very hairs of your
head are all numbered.*

MATTHEW 10:30

Some people wondered if God had forgotten about them because God had promised them Jesus but Jesus hadn't shown up yet. The people did not have to worry. God had not forgotten them. One of the amazing things about God is that He knows everything about everybody all the time, and that kind of knowing helps God make choices that are perfectly right.

God chose Jesus' mother, Mary, from among all the women in the world. And He chose Joseph to be Jesus' daddy on earth from all the world's men. Of all the places in the world, God chose the little town of Bethlehem as the place where Jesus would be born. He chose the exact day of Jesus' birth and the exact time. God's plan was coming together in a perfect way.

Do you believe that God knows everything about you? He chose your mom and dad and where and when you would be born. He chose the colors of your skin, eyes, and hair. God even chose how many hairs would be on your head! Can you count them all? God can. He knows exactly how many there are.

Dear Father, thank You for always choosing what is best for me. Thank You for remembering me and knowing everything about me.

GOD GIVE YE MERRY CHRISTMAS TIDE

God give ye merry Christmas tide,
Ye gentle people all!
And in your merry making may
No evil chance befall:
Rejoice! for once at Bethlehem,
While shepherds knelt to pray,

Chorus:

Our blessed Master Jesus Christ,

Was born on Christmas Day;

Our blessed Master Jesus Christ,

Was born on Christmas Day.

OLD ENGLISH CAROL

Choosing a Name

For unto us a child is born, unto us a son is given: and the government shall be upon his shoulder: and his name shall be called Wonderful, Counsellor, The mighty God, The everlasting Father, The Prince of Peace.

ISAIAH 9:6

Before a baby is born, that baby's parents spend a lot of time choosing a name for their child. A name is important, for it will stay with that child throughout life. Often, the parents will choose a name that reflects a positive character trait. Or perhaps they will name their child after someone they admire.

When Jesus was born, He was given many names. Each name tells us something about who He is. He is called Wonderful because He *is* wonderful. He is called Counselor because He helps us to make good choices.

Jesus is the Mighty God. He is not beneath God—He *is* God! He is the Everlasting Father. Even those who don't have a father here on earth can claim Jesus as their Father. He will never stop being Father to all who ask.

He is the Prince of Peace. Even when things are scary and unsettled, we can know peace if we know Jesus.

Jesus has many more names, as well. Each name tells us how great He is. Each one lets us know how much He loves us.

Dear Father, thank You for giving Jesus many names, so we could know more about Him. Help me to know and remember all the wonderful things about Him.

Hark! The Herald Angels Sing

Hail, the Heav'n-born Prince of Peace!
Hail the Sun of righteousness!
Light and life to all He brings,
Ris'n with healing in His wings;
Mild He lays His glory by,
Born that man no more may die;
Born to raise the sons of earth;
Born to give them second birth.

Come, Desire of nations, come!

Fix in us Thy humble home;

Rise, the woman's conqu'ring seed,

Bruise in us the serpent's head;

Adam's likeness now efface,

Stamp Thine image in its place;

Second Adam from above,

Reinstate us in Thy love.

CHARLES WESLEY

Rules

And it came to pass in those days,
that there went out a decree from Caesar
Augustus that all the world
should be taxed.

LUKE 2:1

Finally, God's plan was ready. It was time to send Jesus to earth. While most of God's people were waiting and wondering, God was busy. He had chosen Mary and Joseph as Jesus' earthly parents. He had planned where and when Jesus would be born. Now, God had one more thing to do. He had to get Mary and Joseph to the little town of Bethlehem. They did not live there. They lived in a place called Nazareth about 80 miles away.

So, God whispered to the emperor's heart (the emperor was a leader, like a king), "Everyone must go to the city where they were born so all the people can be counted and pay their taxes." And that is exactly what the emperor did. He made a rule, and Mary and Joseph had to follow it. They had to go to Bethlehem.

When God makes rules, He expects His children to obey them. Are you a good rule follower? Can you name some important rules?

Dear Father, I know that rules are important. Rules keep me safe, and they help me to learn. Help me, please, to follow the rules.

O LITTLE TOWN OF BETHLEHEM

O little town of Bethlehem,
How still we see thee lie;
Above thy deep and dreamless sleep
The silent stars go by:

Yet in thy dark streets shineth
The everlasting Light;
The hopes and fears of all the years
Are met in thee tonight.

PHILLIPS BROOKS

God with Us

Now all this was done, that it might be fulfilled which was spoken of the Lord by the prophet, saying, Behold, a virgin shall be with child, and shall bring forth a son, and they shall call his name Emmanuel, which being interpreted is, God with us.

MATTHEW 1:22–23

God had promised His people that His Son was coming to be their king. For a long, long time, they had looked forward to Jesus' arrival. They had waited and hoped and prayed. It had been so long, some of them wondered if it was ever going to happen!

But God gave them signs to look for, so they would know Jesus was really God's Son. They were to look for a young girl who was going to have a baby. She would name her son, "Immanuel," which means, "God with us." When those things happened, they would know that God had kept His promise.

When Jesus was born, God truly did come to live with us. Instead of being in heaven where no one could see Him, He became a man. People could now talk to God and touch God and hug God and laugh with God. Because Jesus is God, the people were able to be with Him. When Jesus came, God was really with us!

Jesus was with the people when He was born. Today, God is still with us, watching over us and caring for us. He is all around us, and we can talk to Him any time. He promises to never, ever leave us.

Dear Father, thank You for choosing to be with us. I know I can talk to You any time, and You will never leave me.

HARK! THE HERALD ANGELS SING

Christ, by highest heaven adored,
Christ, the everlasting Lord:
Late in time, behold Him come,
Offspring of a virgin's womb.

Veiled in flesh the Godhead see,

Hail the incarnate Deity!

Pleased as man with men to dwell,

Jesus our Emmanuel.

CHARLES WESLEY

Travelers

And Joseph also went up from Galilee,
out of the city of Nazareth, into Judaea,
unto the city of David, which is called
Bethlehem; (because he was of the house
and lineage of David:) to be taxed
with Mary his espoused wife,
being great with child.

LUKE 2:4–5

Mary and Joseph lived in a time when there were no cars, trains, or airplanes. They walked all the way to Bethlehem. Walking was hard for Mary because Baby Jesus was about to be born. Do you wonder if she and Joseph worried? What if Mary had the baby somewhere between home and Bethlehem? What if there was no one to help when the baby came?

But Mary and Joseph did not have to worry. God's angels had visited both of them, and those angels told them about their special baby. Mary and Joseph did not have to worry because God was with them all the way to Bethlehem. He protected them and little Baby Jesus, who had not yet been born.

God also goes with you wherever *you* go. You can't see Him, but He is always there. God stays with you all the time, keeping you safe and sound.

Dear Father, thank You for staying with me.
I like knowing that wherever I go You
are with me. I like that You always
keep me safe and sound.

O Come, All Ye Faithful

O come, all ye faithful, joyful
and triumphant!
O come ye, O come ye
to Bethlehem;
Come and behold him
Born the King of angels:
O come, let us adore Him,
O come, let us adore Him,
O come, let us adore Him,
Christ the Lord.

Sing, choirs of angels, sing in exultation,
Sing, all ye citizens of heaven above!
Glory to God in the highest:
O come, let us adore Him,
O come, let us adore Him,
O come, let us adore Him,
Christ the Lord.

JOHN FRANCIS WADE

Anything Is Possible

*For with God nothing
shall be impossible.*

LUKE 1:37

Mary didn't understand how she could be the mother of God's son. It didn't seem possible to her. It just didn't make any sense, and she felt confused.

"Don't be confused," the angel said to her. "God can do anything." Then, he told Mary that her cousin, Elizabeth, was going to have a baby, too. Elizabeth was very old, and had never had any children before. It seemed impossible for Elizabeth to have a baby at her age. But God made it happen.

Mary accepted the angel's explanation. She still didn't understand, but she knew that God could do anything. She chose to trust Him, even though it didn't make sense to her. "Okay," she said. "I'll do whatever God wants me to do."

Sometimes, things don't make sense to us. We don't always understand what God is doing. But even when we feel confused, we can trust God. He loves us, and He has great plans for us. He can do anything—nothing is impossible with God. No matter what, we can choose to be like Mary. We can say, "Even though I don't understand, I'll do whatever God wants me to do. I will trust God."

Dear Father, I'm glad to know that nothing is impossible for You. When I feel confused, help me to remember that I can still trust You. When things don't make sense to me, I can trust that You know what You are doing, and You will take care of me.

I Wonder as I Wander

If Jesus had wanted for any wee thing
A star in the sky or a bird on the wing
Or all of God's Angels in heaven to sing
He surely could have it,
'cause he was the King

I wonder as I wander out under the sky
How Jesus the Saviour did come for
to die For poor orn'ry people like
you and like I; I wonder as I
wander out under the sky

Traditional Appalachian Carol

A Place to Stay

Blessed be the Lord:
for he hath shewed me his marvellous
kindness in a strong city.

PSALM 31:21

When Mary and Joseph arrived, they must have seen that Bethlehem was filled with people. In just a few days, the Little Town of Bethlehem had become the Busy Town of Bethlehem. Like Joseph, everyone had returned to his hometown to be counted and pay taxes.

When Mary and Joseph looked for a place to stay, all the rooms were taken. But they did not have to worry, because God had a plan.

A kind innkeeper knew where they could stay. Some people believe they stayed in a stable. Others think it was a cave. But where Mary and Joseph stayed is not as important as God's plan for them. He already knew where Jesus would be born—in a simple place among the animals. And when Baby Jesus came, Mary wrapped Him up, all toasty warm, and laid Him in a manger. (A manger is a long, open box for farm animals to eat from.)

Kind people, like the innkeeper in the story, are God's special helpers. How was the innkeeper kind? How can you be kind to others?

Dear Father, You are always so kind to me!
Let me be Your special helper.
Teach me to be kind to others.

Away in a Manger

Away in a manger,
no crib for His bed,
The little Lord Jesus laid down
His sweet head;
The stars in the sky looked
down where He lay,
The little Lord Jesus,
asleep in the hay.

The cattle are lowing,
the poor Baby wakes.
But little Lord Jesus,
no crying He makes.
I love Thee, Lord Jesus,
look down from the sky.
And stay by the cradle
till morning is nigh.

Be near me, Lord Jesus,
I ask Thee to stay
Close by me forever,
and love me, I pray!
Bless all the dear children
in Thy tender care
And take us to heaven,
to live with Thee there.

UNKNOWN

Regular Person

And Mary said, My soul doth magnify the
Lord, and my spirit hath rejoiced in God
my Saviour. For he hath regarded the
low estate of his handmaiden.

LUKE 1:46–48

When Mary realized that she had been chosen to be the mother of God's Son, she was amazed! She couldn't believe that the God of the universe had chosen her, a young girl, to do such a big job.

She probably thought, *Why did He choose me? I've never done anything important. I'm still young. There are plenty of older, smarter, richer, more important girls. . . . I'm just a regular person. Why didn't He choose someone else?*

But God doesn't look for the important people to do His work. He wants regular people, just like you and me. He wants men and women and boys and girls who live normal lives and work hard and try their best at school. He wants people who love Him and who want to do what He says.

God chose Mary, a young girl, to be the mother of His Son. He chooses you and me to do His important work, as well. Like Mary, we can be excited and amazed, knowing that God notices us, He sees us as important, and He believes we can do His work.

Dear Father, thank You for giving me important work to do. I feel honored that You have chosen me to do special things for you. I will do whatever You ask me to. I love You.

THE ANGEL GABRIEL FROM HEAVEN CAME

Then gentle Mary meekly
bowed her head,
"To me be as it pleaseth God,"
she said, "My soul shall laud
and magnify His holy Name."
Most highly favored lady, Gloria!

Of her, Emmanuel, the Christ,
was born In Bethlehem,
all on a Christmas morn,
And Christian folk throughout
the world will ever say—
"Most highly favored lady,"
Gloria!

BASQUE CAROL
TRANSLATED BY SABINE BARING-GOULD

Silent night

Be silent, O all flesh, before the Lord:
for he is raised up out
of his holy habitation.

ZECHARIAH 2:13

Mary and Joseph knew that Baby Jesus was the One God had promised to send, but no one else in Bethlehem knew. At that very minute when Jesus was born, no one was waiting for Him to come. Most people were sound asleep in their beds not knowing that something wonderful had just happened. The night was starry and silent except for the sound of a baby crying.

But God was there. He was there on that silent night watching over Baby Jesus, Mary, Joseph, and all the people in the world. God's plan was unfolding, and He was about to do something big. God was about to send some special messengers down to earth.

Do you know that God is with you all through the night? He is! Just as He was with Baby Jesus on that night long ago, God is with you, too. God never sleeps. When you are sound asleep in your bed and the night is dark and your house is silent, God is right there watching over you. Isn't that wonderful?

Dear Father, bless me as I sleep tonight. Be with my family and me. And please give us a good night's sleep and many happy dreams.

Silent Night

Silent night! Holy night!
All is calm, all is bright,
Round yon Virgin Mother and Child!
Holy Infant, so tender and mild,
Sleep in heavenly peace!
Sleep in heavenly peace!

Silent night! Holy night!
Sleeps the world in peace tonight.
God sends His Son to earth below,
A Child from whom all blessings flow.
Jesus embraces mankind.
Jesus embraces mankind.

JOSEPH MOHR

Good Citizens

*And it came to pass in those days,
that there went out a decree from Caesar
Augustus that all the world should be
taxed. . . . And all went to be taxed,
every one into his own city.*

LUKE **2:1, 3**

Caesar Augustus was the emperor of the Roman Empire. He wanted to know how many people lived in his kingdom. Every few years, he made all the people go to their hometowns so they could be counted.

At that time, travelers packed up enough belongings for a long trip. The people who still lived in their hometowns didn't have far to go. But if anyone had moved away, he or she had to pack food and water and clothes to last for many days.

When they got to their hometowns, they registered and told how many people were in their families. This way, Caesar would know how many people lived in his kingdom. He used this information for all sorts of things. It helped him know how many taxes to collect, how many guards to hire, how many roads to build, and other things.

It is important for us to do what our government asks us to do, as long as they don't ask us to disobey God. Governments help countries and kingdoms run more smoothly. God wants us to obey the laws and be good citizens.

Dear Father, thank you for placing people in charge of my government who want to help take care of me. Please give them wisdom as they work to try and make my home a good and safe place to live.

AUGUSTUS CAESAR HAVING BROUGHT

Augustus Caesar having brought
The world to quiet peace,
That all the noise of bloody wars
In every land did cease;
Just Joseph, with his Mary mild,
To Bethlehem did come,
Which blessed place appointed was
To ease her burden'd womb

Then, all the town being full of guests,
Such was their helpless case,
That not a bed for them was left,
Nor any lodging place;
But in a poor and simple inn,
Even an ox's stall
Appointed was to entertain
The Saviour of us all.

O sing we all, with heart and voice,
Let Christian love increase,
For unto us this day is born
The only Prince of Peace.

DAVIES GILBERT

Shepherds

And there were in the same country
shepherds abiding in the field,
keeping watch over their flock by night.
And, lo, the angel of the Lord came
upon them, and the glory of the Lord
shone round about them:
and they were sore afraid.

Luke 2:8–9

Near Bethlehem that night, in the fields, shepherds watched their flocks of sheep. A shepherd's job is to care for his sheep, so God knew the shepherds would be awake. He sent them an angel. The angel came in a very bright light. At first the shepherds were afraid, but the angel told them, "Do not be afraid! I have come to give you Good News. A baby was born tonight in Bethlehem. He is the One God promised would come to save the world." The angel told the shepherds where to find Jesus, and then— the sky filled up with angels praising God!

God surprised the shepherds with Good News brought by angels. God likes surprising His people with wonderful things. These gifts from God are called blessings. Jesus is the best blessing of all because He came to show us the way to heaven. What other blessings can you think of?

Dear Father, thank You for sending us
Jesus. He is the best blessing of all.
And thank You for my family, my home,
and all of Your blessings!

WHILE SHEPHERDS WATCHED THEIR FLOCKS

While shepherds watch'd their flocks
by night, all seated on the ground,
The angel of the Lord came down,
And glory shone around.
And glory shone around.

"To you in David's town this day
Is born of David's line,
A Savior, which is Christ the Lord;
And this shall be the sign.
And this shall be the sign."

"The heav'nly Babe you there shall find
To human view display'd.
All meanly wrapped in
swaddling bands,
And in a manger laid.
And in a manger laid."

NAHUM TATE

Trust and Obey

*And Joseph also went up from Galilee,
out of the city of Nazareth, into Judaea,
unto the city of David, which is called
Bethlehem; (because he was of the
house and lineage of David:) to be taxed
with Mary his espoused wife,
being great with child.*

Luke 2:4–5

Mary and Joseph's families had moved away from their hometown, a place called Bethlehem. Now they lived in the town of Nazareth. Mary and Joseph had to pack up their things and make the long journey back to Bethlehem, so they could be counted. They wanted to be good citizens, so they obeyed their emperor.

It was close to time for Mary to give birth to Jesus, but that didn't matter. She still had to go to Bethlehem to be counted. It was probably a difficult journey for her. She may have wondered why God would ask her to do such a hard thing. But she didn't fuss or complain. She did what she was asked to do. She trusted that God had a reason for making her take that long trip.

Dear Father, sometimes I have to do things I don't want to do. At times, I have to work when I'd rather play, or I have to go to sleep when I want to stay awake. Sometimes I have to take long trips, and sitting in the car for hours isn't fun. Help me to have a sweet attitude. Help me to trust You, even when I don't understand.

O Little Town of Bethlehem

How silently, how silently
The wondrous gift is given!
So God imparts to human hearts
The blessings of His heaven.
No ear may hear His coming,
But in this world of sin,
Where meek souls will receive him still,
The dear Christ enters in.

O holy Child of Bethlehem
Descend to us, we pray
Cast out our sin and enter in
Be born to us today
We hear the Christmas angels
The great glad tidings tell
O come to us, abide with us
Our Lord Emmanuel

PHILLIPS BROOKS

The Star

When they saw the star,
they rejoiced with exceeding great joy.

MATTHEW 2:10

On that silent, dark night when Jesus was born, God brought light into the world. The angels came to the shepherds in a big burst of light. But that was not all God did. He put a bright star up in the sky right above Jesus. That bright star, Jesus' star, could be seen from far away. God did not want to keep the Good News about Jesus a secret. He wanted people near and far to know that Jesus had come to the world. The big, bright star would lead them to where Jesus was.

God is in charge of everything. He made the sky and everything in it. So, when God wanted a new star to appear, He made it happen. Do you know that God named all the stars? He knows each one. And, even better, He made you and He knows you. God knows everyone—all the people who have ever lived on earth, all the people who live here now, and all the people who will live here in the future. That is how great and wonderful God is!

Dear Father, I think it is special that You made the sky and know all the stars. And I think it is really special that You made and know me.

STAR OF BETHLEHEM, SWEETLY SHINING

Star of Bethlehem, sweetly shining,
Let thy peaceful light
Lead us where the Christ is lying,

On this Christmas night.

Hail, sweet Jesus, ever blest,

Pearl of sweetness unexpress'd.

A. S. WOODS

Mary's Donkey

Joseph also went up. . .to be taxed
with Mary his espoused wife,
being great with child.

Luke 2:4–5

Clop, clop, clop. The donkey's hooves played a rhythm on the rocky road. Perhaps Mary hummed songs to the rhythm. Perhaps she heard a lullaby and dozed during the long journey.

Bethlehem was a long distance from Nazareth. It took four or five days to travel there, and the roads were rocky and hilly. Most people traveled in groups for safety, because there were often robbers along the trail.

Because Mary was expecting Jesus, it would have been difficult for her to make the journey on foot. She probably rode a donkey. Perhaps she gave him a name and fed him treats. She was probably very grateful for the donkey because, without him, she would have had to walk the entire way.

What a special job that donkey had, carrying God's Son and His mother! That simple donkey played an important role in God's special plan. God had a plan for Mary, for Joseph, and even for the donkey. He has a plan for you, too. He loves you, and wants you to honor Him by doing your best in everything.

Dear Father, thank You for taking care of
Mary on the long journey to Bethlehem.
Thank You for sending us animals to love and
care for. Mary's donkey gave his best for you.
I want to always give my best for You, too.

THE FRIENDLY BEASTS

Jesus our brother, kind and good
Was humbly born in a stable rude
And the friendly beasts around Him stood,
Jesus our brother, kind and good.

"I," said the donkey, shaggy and brown,
"I carried His mother up hill and down;
I carried her safely to Bethlehem town."
"I," said the donkey, shaggy and brown.

TRADITIONAL ENGLISH CAROL

Angels

For he shall give his angels charge over
thee, to keep thee in all thy ways.

PSALM 91:11

Angels are God's special messengers. Almost a year before Jesus was born, God sent an angel to Mary. This angel, named Gabriel, surprised Mary. He told her that God had chosen her to be Jesus' mother. Can you imagine how Mary must have felt? Gabriel told her that the baby's name should be "Jesus." Then God sent another angel to Joseph in a dream. That angel told Joseph to be a good husband to Mary.

Angels played a big part in the Christmas story—the story of Jesus' birthday. They were there the night Jesus was born. They shared the Good News with the shepherds, and they sang songs of joy.

Today God still sends angels to earth to do His work. Angels are all around, but you cannot see them. God promised to send His angels to watch over His people, and God always keeps His promises. Right now, His angels are busy working. Do you know what they are doing? They are watching over you!

Dear Father, I feel good knowing that Your angels are all around me all the time. Thank You for sending them to watch over me.

ANGELS WE HAVE HEARD ON HIGH

Angels we have heard on high
Sweetly singing o'er the plains,
And the mountains in reply
Echoing their joyous strains.

Chorus:
Gloria, in excelsis Deo!
Gloria, in excelsis Deo!

Come to Bethlehem and see
Him whose birth the angels sing;
Come, adore on bended knee,
Christ the Lord, the newborn King.

TRADITIONAL FRENCH CAROL

A Promise Is Forever

[God said to David,] And thine house and thy kingdom shall be established for ever before thee: thy throne shall be established for ever.

When David was a little boy, he was a lot like all little boys. He helped his family take care of their animals. He liked to play with rocks, and he practiced throwing them at targets. He enjoyed music, and he often sang songs to God.

God liked David, and He thought David would make a good king. He promised David that he would be king one day. But it was a long time before that promise came true. While he was waiting, David might have wondered if God was ever going to keep His promise. But God always keeps His promises, and one day, David became the king.

God promised David that his kingdom would last forever. But it was a long, long time before God made that promise come true. Long after David's death, David's great-great-great (many greats) grandson was born. That baby's name was Jesus. He was in David's family, but He was also God's Son. Through Jesus, God kept His promise to David. Jesus was the king, and He is still the king today. His kingdom will last forever.

God has made promises to us, too. He promises

to never leave us. He promises to love us and care for us. And He promises that, if we believe in Jesus, we will spend eternity with Him in heaven. At times, we may wonder if God is going to keep His promises to us. But we never have to wonder about that. God kept His promises to David, and He will keep His promises to us.

Dear Father, thank You for all the promises You gave us. Thank You for always keeping Your promises.

COME, THOU LONG-EXPECTED JESUS

Come, Thou long expected Jesus,
Born to set Thy people free;
From our fears and sins release us,
Let us find our rest in Thee.
Israel's Strength and Consolation,
Hope of all the earth Thou art;
Dear Desire of every nation,
Joy of every longing heart.

Born Thy people to deliver,

Born a child and yet a King,

Born to reign in us forever,

Now Thy gracious kingdom bring.

By Thine own eternal Spirit

Rule in all our hearts alone;

By Thine all sufficient merit,

Raise us to Thy glorious throne.

CHARLES WESLEY

Baby Jesus

For unto us a child is born, unto us a son is given: and the government shall be upon his shoulder: and his name shall be called Wonderful, Counsellor, The mighty God, The everlasting Father, The Prince of Peace.

Isaiah 9:6

If you had seen Baby Jesus on the night He was born, you would have thought He looked like any other baby. But Jesus was a very special baby. There never had been and there never will be another baby like Him.

Baby Jesus was God's own Son. He was God Himself come down to the earth in a human body. Baby Jesus was perfect in every way. And when He grew up, Jesus would keep on being perfect. He would say and do things to amaze people, things that only God can do.

Jesus is the world's great heavenly King, and today He sits in heaven on a throne right next to God's. Someday when you get to heaven, you will see Jesus all grown up. And He will be happy to see you. One of the many wonderful things about Jesus is that He is with you all the time, now and forever. Why? Because Jesus loves you!

Dear Jesus, I feel happy that You came down to earth, and I am happy that I will see You one day. Thank You for loving me. I love You, too!

A Boy Is Born in Bethlehem!

A Boy is born in Bethlehem!
Alleluia! Alleluia!
And joy is in Jerusalem,
Alleluia! Alleluia!

Therefore let us with one accord,

Alleluia! Alleluia!

On this His birthday praise the Lord!

Alleluia! Alleluia!

14TH-CENTURY LATIN HYMN

No Room

There was no room
for them in the inn.

LUKE 2:7

Bethlehem was very crowded. Everyone in all the surrounding towns had walked or ridden their donkeys to Bethlehem so they could be counted. Only the first people there were able to find hotel rooms. The others had to sleep outside on the ground. Some of them may have slept in tents.

Joseph wanted Mary to have a warm place to stay. He knew the baby would be born soon, and he didn't want the baby to be born in the cold, windy night air. "Please, sir, can you find a place for us?" he asked the busy innkeeper. He knew how crowded it was, but he was hoping that someone would see that Mary was going to have a baby soon and make room for her.

The kind innkeeper looked at Mary. He wanted to help, but all his rooms were taken! He couldn't kick out any of his customers. After all, they were there first. He didn't know what to do.

Then, he had an idea. "Come with me," he said. "You can stay in my stable. At least it's warm there." He led them to where he kept his animals. It smelled of hay, and the animals probably made noises.

"Baaaa!" said the sheep.

"Mooooo!" said the cow.

Joseph led Mary into the warm stable. He made her comfortable in the hay and thanked God for taking care of his family.

Dear Father, thank You for always taking care of us. Even when things don't go exactly as we planned, we know You are watching over us.

Thou Didst Leave Thy Throne

Thou didst leave Thy throne
and Thy kingly crown,
When Thou camest to Earth for me;
But in Bethlehem's home was
there found no room
For Thy holy nativity.

O come to my heart, Lord Jesus,

There is room in my heart for Thee.

My heart shall rejoice, Lord Jesus,

When Thou comest and callest for me.

EMILY E. S. ELLIOTT

And the shepherds returned,
glorifying and praising God for all
the things that they had heard
and seen, as it was told unto them.

LUKE 2:20

When the angels appeared to shepherds in the fields, they praised God. Do you know what "praise" means? Praise is when you say something to God that shows you respect, appreciate, and love Him. "I love You, God!" "You are so great." "Thank You for blessing me." Those are a few things that you could say to praise God.

After the angels told the shepherds about Jesus, the shepherds hurried to find the baby boy. When they found him, they praised Him. The shepherds knew that Baby Jesus was a special gift from God. And when they went back to the fields with their sheep, the shepherds praised God all the way. They thanked Him for what the angels told them. They thanked Him for Jesus and for all the wonderful things they saw that night.

You should praise God, too. God loves it when His children praise Him. Praise Him because He loves You. Praise Him for all the wonderful things He does. Praise Him just because He is God.

Dear God, You are so wonderful!
Thank You for all the ways that You
bless me. I praise You for being
the one and only God.

PRAISE GOD THE LORD, YE SONS OF MEN

Praise God the Lord, ye sons of men,
Before His highest throne;
Today He opens heaven again
And gives us His own Son.
And gives us His own Son.

He leaves His heavenly Father's throne,

Is born an infant small,

And in a manger, poor and lone,

Lies in a humble stall.

Lies in a humble stall.

W. Nikolaus Herman

It's Time!

And so it was, that, while they were there,
the days were accomplished
that she should be delivered.

LUKE 2:6

Joseph and Mary made themselves comfortable in the soft hay of the stable. They may have made friends with the animals there, talking to them and giving them names. Perhaps Mary's own donkey stayed in the stable with them.

Before long, Mary looked at Joseph. "I think it's time," she told him. It was time for Jesus to be born. Since this was their first child, Mary may have felt afraid. Perhaps there was a woman nearby—maybe the innkeeper's wife—who had been through this before. Perhaps she helped Mary to stay calm.

Joseph may have helped, too, or he may have paced back and forth nervously, praying that his wife and the baby would be okay. But he didn't need to worry. The baby who was about to be born was God's Son. God would take care of them.

God's Son, Jesus, was the King of Kings. God could have chosen for His Son to be born anywhere. He could have been born in a huge mansion or a palace. But He wasn't born in any fancy place. He was born in a stable, surrounded by hay and animals. God chose for Jesus to be born in a place where anybody and everybody could find Him.

Dear Father, thank You for sending Your Son as a gift to the world. You didn't hide Him from us, or make it difficult for us to find Him. You promised that everyone who looks for Him will find Him. Thank You for Jesus.

SILENT NIGHT! HOLY NIGHT!

Silent night, holy night,
Son of God, love's pure light.
Radiant beams from Thy holy face,
With the dawn of redeeming grace,
Jesus, Lord at Thy birth,
Jesus, Lord, at Thy birth.

Silent night, holy night,
Wondrous star, lend thy light;
With the angels let us sing,
Alleluia to our King;
Christ the Savior is born.
Christ the Savior is born.

JOSEPH MOHR

The Wise Men

Now when Jesus was born in Bethlehem of Judaea in the days of Herod the king, behold, there came wise men from the east to Jerusalem, saying, Where is he that is born King of the Jews? for we have seen his star in the east, and are come to worship him.

Matthew 2:1–2

After Jesus was born, men traveled a long way to see Him. These men were powerful leaders who enjoyed studying the stars. When they saw Jesus' star, they wanted to follow it so they could find Him. They wanted to praise and worship Jesus and bring Him gifts. These men were very wise. Along with many other things, they knew that the stars in the sky would help them find their way. They knew that certain stars pointed north, south, east, and west. And they knew that following the biggest, brightest star would lead them to Jesus.

Being wise means being smart. Wisdom comes from God. You become wise by learning, and if you ask God He will help you to learn. Learning about God is important. Learning His ways will make you wise like the wise men. Then you can share your wisdom with others.

Dear Father, I want to be wise, so help me to learn. I know that learning is important. Teach me Your ways so I can share them with my family and friends.

WE THREE KINGS OF ORIENT ARE

We three kings of Orient are
Bearing gifts we traverse afar.
Field and fountain, moor and mountain,
Following yonder star.

Chorus:

O Star of wonder, star of night,

Star with royal beauty bright,

Westward leading, still proceeding,

Guide us to thy perfect Light.

JOHN HENRY HOPKINS

Safe and Warm

And she brought forth her firstborn son,
and wrapped him in swaddling clothes,
and laid him in a manger.

LUKE 2:7

Every day, new babies are born all over the world. Every day, the mommies count the tiny fingers and toes of their babies and admire their sweet faces. Then, they wrap the babies tightly in blankets and hold them close. Babies like to be bundled in warm blankets. It makes them feel safe.

Baby Jesus was no different from other babies. His mommy probably counted His fingers and toes. She probably exclaimed over how beautiful and perfect He was. Then, she wrapped Him in soft cloths, or small blankets, and held Him close. Maybe she sang to Him as she fed Him. Perhaps she watched Him fall asleep, then placed Him in a manger.

A manger was a feeding trough for the animals. There was no fancy cradle in the stable, so Joseph may have put fresh hay in the manger. Maybe he laid a clean blanket on top of the hay, to make a soft place for Baby Jesus. Then Mary laid him there. She and Joseph probably sat and looked at Him for a long time, thanking God for giving them a strong, healthy boy.

God provided a warm place for Jesus to be born. He provided a soft place for Jesus to sleep. It may not have been fancy, but it was all He needed. God provides what we need, too.

Dear Father, thank You for always giving me what I need. Help me to be thankful for the good things You give.

WHILE SHEPHERDS WATCHED THEIR FLOCKS

The heavenly Babe you there shall find
To human view displayed,
All meanly wrapped in swathing bands,
And in a manger laid;
And in a manger laid.

Thus spake the seraph and forthwith
Appeared a shining throng
Of angels, praising God, and thus
Addressed their joyful song:
"All glory be to God on high,
And to the earth be peace;
Good will henceforth from
Heaven to men
Begin and never cease
begin and never cease."

NAHUM TATE

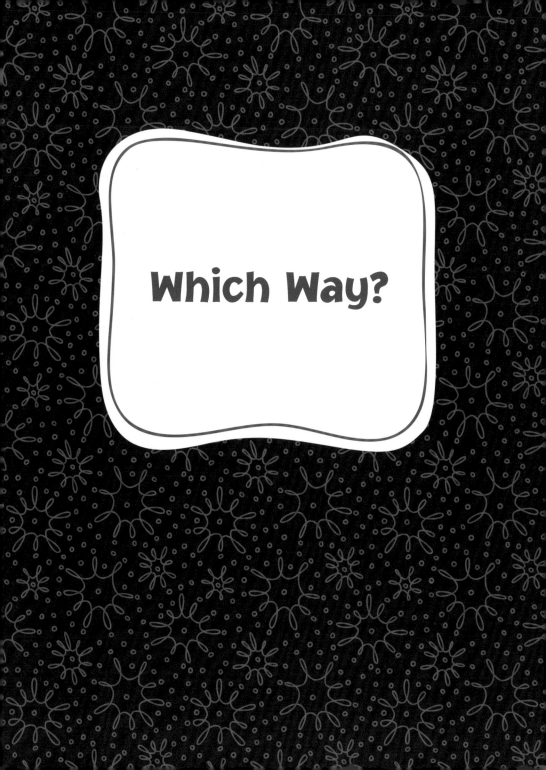

Which Way?

*Ask, and it shall be given you; seek,
and ye shall find; knock, and it shall be
opened unto you: for every one that
asketh receiveth; and he that seeketh
findeth; and to him that knocketh
it shall be opened.*

MATTHEW 7:7–8

As smart as the wise men were, they still stopped and asked for directions. In a city called Jerusalem they asked its king, a man named Herod, for help. They said, "Where is he that is born King of the Jews? for we have seen his star in the east, and are come to worship him" (Matthew 2:2).

The king did not know where Jesus was, so he called his men together and asked if they knew. Some had heard of God's promise to send Someone to save the world. Others knew that Jesus would be born in Bethlehem. So, King Herod told the wise men to go to Bethlehem to search for Jesus.

Whenever you need directions, you can ask someone to help you. You can ask God. He knows everything. When you pray and ask God what to do, He promises to show you the way—and His way is always right.

Dear Father, sometimes I can't make up my mind about what to do. Remind me that I can always ask You, and You will show me the way.

WHEN CHRIST WAS BORN IN BETHLEHEM

When Christ was born in Bethlehem,
'Twas night, but seemed the noon of day;
The stars, whose light
Was pure and bright,
Shone with unwavering ray;

But one, one glorious star
Guided the Eastern Magi from afar.

ALPHONSUS MARIA DE LIGUORI

The Gift in the Manger

She. . .wrapped him in swaddling clothes,
and laid him in a manger; because there
was no room for them in the inn.

Luke 2:7

Chomp, chomp, chomp. The donkeys crunched on the hay filling the manger.

"Baaaa!" a sheep nudged his way in, claiming some of the meal for himself.

Little did the animals know, later that night their feeding trough would hold a great treasure.

When Jesus was born, Mary needed a soft place to lay him. Because they were in a stable, there were no fancy cradles. She didn't want to lay him on the ground—he might get stepped on!

"Here, honey. We can lay Jesus in this manger," Joseph may have said. The hay provided a soft cushion, and it kept Him safe from animals' hooves.

Who would have thought that the King of Kings would make his bed in a smelly old feeding trough? This proves that you cannot judge a gift by its package. After all, Jesus was God's most precious gift to the world. And God didn't choose to wrap Him in an expensive, sparkly package. Instead, Jesus was wrapped in simple cloths, and He slept in a manger.

Sometimes, the best gifts are the ones that come in simple packages. They may lack sparkle, but they are filled with love. Those are the gifts that will last and last, even after the package has been discarded.

Dear Father, thank You for the gift
of Your love. Thank You, also,
for the reminder that Your best
gifts often come in simple packages.

AWAY IN A MANGER

Away in a manger,
no crib for a bed,
The little Lord Jesus laid
down His sweet head.
The stars in the sky looked
down where He lay—
The little Lord Jesus,
asleep on the hay.

The cattle are lowing,
the poor baby wakes,
But little Lord Jesus,
no crying He makes;
I love Thee, Lord Jesus!
Look down from the sky,
And stay by my cradle
till morning is nigh.

SOMETIMES ATTRIBUTED TO MARTIN LUTHER

King Herod

*Behold, the angel of the Lord appeareth
to Joseph in a dream, saying, Arise,
and take the young child and his mother,
and flee into Egypt, and be thou there
until I bring thee word: for Herod will
seek the young child to destroy him.*

MATTHEW 2:13

Another name for Jesus is King of the Jews. There will never be another king as great as He. But not every king is good. King Herod was a bad king. He wanted all the power, and he was jealous of Baby Jesus. He did not like it that God wanted Jesus to grow up and lead the people.

So Herod made an awful plan. He planned to kill Baby Jesus. But God was not going to let that happen! He sent an angel to warn Joseph. Then Joseph took Mary and Jesus to a place called Egypt, and they stayed there until it was safe to go home.

God wants the world ruled by good leaders. Someday when you are old enough, you can help decide who your leaders should be. But for now, you can do this: you can pray for leaders everywhere.

Dear Father, I pray that all the world's leaders will love You and follow Your rules. And thank You, God, for making Jesus the one great King.

THE CHILDREN'S KING

No courtiers greet His birth await,
Though He is King of glory,
But through the sky the angels fly
To tell the wondrous story.

Chorus:
The children's King,
the children's King,
O come let us adore Him;
Our carols bring,
His praises sing,
All kneeling low before Him.

When told His name,
the shepherds came
Where that dear Babe was sleeping;
We haste with them to Bethlehem,
Our happy Christmas keeping.

UNKNOWN

Doing Their Jobs

And there were in the same country
shepherds abiding in the field,
keeping watch over
their flock by night.

LUKE 2:8

A shepherd's job is to take care of sheep. It isn't an easy job, for sheep need to be watched all day and all night long, every single day. If a shepherd doesn't do his job, one of the sheep might wander off and get lost or hurt.

There are many dangers to sheep, especially if they become separated from the rest of the flock. They might fall off a cliff and break a bone. Wolves might attack them. Being a shepherd is a demanding job.

On the night Jesus was born, some shepherds were nearby watching over their flocks. Some of the shepherds may have thought, *I'm tired. I don't want to watch over these silly old sheep. Why can't they take care of themselves? I want to go home and go to bed*. But we should always do our jobs, even when we don't feel like it. When we obey God and do what we are supposed to do, He blesses us.

Little did those shepherds know that in a stable nearby, the Son of God was being born. If they had stayed home and not done their jobs that night, they might have missed one of the most exciting nights of their lives!

Dear Father, thank You for blessing me when I obey You. Thank You for giving me important jobs to do. Help me to always do what I'm supposed to do, with a cheerful attitude.

WHILE SHEPHERDS WATCHED THEIR FLOCKS

While shepherds watched
their flocks by night,
All seated on the ground,
The angel of the Lord came down,
And glory shone around,
And glory shone around.

"Fear not!" said he, for mighty dread
Had seized their troubled minds,
"Glad tidings of great joy I bring
To you and all mankind,
To you and all mankind."

NAHUM TATE

Finding Jesus

But sanctify the Lord God in your hearts:
and be ready always to give an answer
to every man that asketh you a reason
of the hope that is in you with
meekness and fear.

1 PETER 3:15

There were no cars, busses, trains, or airplanes in Jesus' time. The wise men walked and rode on camels while they followed the star to Bethlehem. They traveled a long way, in all kinds of weather, through deserts and over hills. Some people think it took the wise men months or even years to find the place where the star shone brightly overhead.

Finding Jesus meant so much to the wise men that they were willing to travel a long way and a long time to get to Him. They knew that Jesus was God's great King, and finding Him was something very special.

Do you know that you can find Jesus, too? You can! And you do not have to travel to find Him. Jesus lives in heaven with God, but He can also live inside your heart—in the place that love comes from. Jesus loves you so much that He will be with you forever.

Dear Jesus, thank You for living inside
my heart and loving me all the time.
I am glad that You were born and
that God sent You to love me.

Jesus Loves Me

Jesus loves me! This I know,
For the Bible tells me so;
Little ones to Him belong;
They are weak, but He is strong.

Chorus:

Yes, Jesus loves me!

Yes, Jesus loves me!

Yes, Jesus loves me!

The Bible tells me so.

ANNA B. WARNER

A Bright Light

And, lo, the angel of the Lord came upon them, and the glory of the Lord shone round about them: and they were sore afraid.

LUKE 2:9

"Baaa, baaa," called the sheep. The shepherds lay on the ground, listening to their flocks and looking up at the stars. Some of them dozed, while others fought to stay awake.

Suddenly, a bright light filled the sky! It lit up the fields and covered the sky as far as they could see.

They placed their arms over their eyes to shield themselves from the bright light. *What in the world is happening,* they must have wondered. *It is the middle of the night! Why is the sky filled with light?*

The light they saw was God's glory. God was happy that His Son had been born, and He wanted the whole world to know. An angel was in the middle of the light. The angel was there as God's messenger, sent to announce Jesus' arrival.

The shepherds were afraid, maybe even terrified! They had never seen anything like this before! Was this a dream? Would the winged creature hurt them? But no, the creature didn't seem angry or mean. It seemed to have something important to tell them. Even the sheep seemed amazed, and they grew quiet.

Although the shepherds were confused, they knew this was a very special night. They looked at the angel, listening for some explanation.

Dear Father, thank You for loving me enough to send Your Son to earth. As I celebrate His birth, help me to be excited about Your love for me.

ANGELS FROM THE REALMS OF GLORY

Angels from the realms of glory,
Wing your flight o'er all the earth;
Ye, who sang creation's story,
Now proclaim Messiah's birth.

Come and worship,
Come and worship,
Worship Christ
The newborn King.

JAMES MONTGOMERY

Treasures

And when they were come into the house, they saw the young child with Mary his mother, and fell down, and worshipped him: and when they had opened their treasures, they presented unto him gifts; gold, and frankincense and myrrh.

Matthew 2:11

When the wise men arrived in Bethlehem, Jesus' star hung in the sky right above the place where He lived. They had found Him!

The wise men had carried precious gifts for Him all the way from the East, treasures called gold, frankincense, and myrrh. These were presents fit for a king. Gold was like money, and frankincense and myrrh were special spices that smelled wonderful. The wise men brought Jesus their most valuable gifts because they knew who He was—God's Son, the great King who would grow up to save the world. The men gave Jesus His gifts, and they knelt down and worshipped Him because they were worshipping God.

If you could give a special gift to Jesus, what would it be? He doesn't expect you to give Him gold, or sweet-smelling spices. Your gift does not have to cost any money. The very best gift you can give Jesus is your love. Love is the greatest gift of all.

Dear Jesus, I have a very special gift for You. This is what it is: I will give You my love today, tomorrow, and forever!

OH, HOW I LOVE JESUS

There is a Name I love to hear,
I love to sing its worth;
It sounds like music in my ear,
The sweetest Name on earth.

Chorus:

Oh, how I love Jesus,

Oh, how I love Jesus,

Oh, how I love Jesus,

Because He first loved me!

FREDERICK WHITFIELD

A Special night

And the angel said unto them, Fear not:
for, behold, I bring you good tidings of
great joy, which shall be to all people.
For unto you is born this day in the city of
David a Saviour, which is Christ the Lord.

Luke 2:10–11

The shepherds had never been so terrified in all their lives. They had been coming to these fields every night for years, and nothing like this had ever happened. Bright lights, winged people in the sky, voices in the air. . .it was unbelievable!

Then the angel spoke to them. "Don't be afraid! I have good news. What I'm about to tell you will make you very happy."

The shepherds watched and listened with their mouths hanging open.

The angel continued. "Today in Bethlehem, God's Son has been born!"

What? How could this be? The shepherds had heard that God was sending a Son. Since they were small children, they had been taught about God's promise to their people. But could this really be true? Could God's own Son—the One their parents and grandparents and great-grandparents had waited for—could He really have been born this night, just over those hills?

The shepherds looked at one another. They wanted to know if the others had seen and heard the same thing. Some of them may have pinched themselves to see if they were dreaming. If what the angel said was true, this was truly a special night!

Dear Father, thank You for sending Your angel to tell the shepherds about Jesus. I want to be like that angel, and share Your good news with everyone.

It Came Upon the Midnight Clear

It came upon the midnight clear,
That glorious song of old,
From angels bending near the earth
To touch their harps of gold:

"Peace on the earth, good-will to men
From heav'n's all-gracious King;"
The world in solemn stillness lay
To hear the angels sing.

EDMUND SEARS

Wonderful Jesus!

For God so loved the world, that he gave his only begotten Son, that whosoever believeth in him should not perish, but have everlasting life.

Jᴏʜɴ 3:16

There are so many wonderful things about Jesus that make Him special. The most important is that Jesus is still here today. You cannot see Him, but He is just as real now as He was on that first Christmas when God sent Him to earth as a baby. Jesus was sent here to love and help people forever.

Jesus is God's Son. He is part of God, and He can do all of the wonderful things that God can do. Best of all, if you believe Jesus came to the world to save people from their sins, Jesus will help you get to heaven someday. And when you get there, you will be with Jesus and God and all the other people who have believed in Him. Heaven is a wonderful, happy place where people live forever. They never die!

Jesus loves children like you. He watches over you every minute of each day, and you can talk to Him whenever you want to just by praying.

What is your favorite thing about Jesus?

Dear Jesus, I like hearing the true story about You when You were a baby. And I love knowing that You are all grown up now and watching over me.

JOY TO THE WORLD!

Joy to the world! The Lord is come.
Let earth receive her King;
Let every heart prepare Him room;
And heav'n and nature sing,
And heav'n and nature sing,
And heav'n and heav'n and nature sing.

He rules the world
with truth and grace,
And makes the nations prove
The glories of His righteousness.
And wonders of His love,
And wonders of His love,
And wonders, wonders of His love.

ISAAC WATTS

Searching
for the King

And this shall be a sign unto you;
ye shall find the babe wrapped in
swaddling clothes, lying in a manger.

Luke 2:12

The shepherds were having a hard time believing their own eyes and ears. Bright lights in the sky? Angels? God's Son, born nearby? It was just too amazing to be true.

The angel must have known they needed a sign. "Go see for yourselves!" the angel told them. "Go to Bethlehem and look for Him. You'll find Him wrapped in cloths and lying in an animal's feeding trough."

Again, the shepherds looked at one another. Why, this story was getting crazier and crazier! A feeding trough? A manger? Why on earth would God send His Son, the Prince of Peace, to be born in a stable? Why would God allow the King of Kings to lie in a smelly, dirty manger?

They jumped to their feet and ran to see for themselves, leaving their sheep behind. Over hills they ran, jumping over rocks and small bushes. Good thing God had sent that bright light, so they could see the path!

Into the center of town they ran, darting in and out of stables, not even caring if they woke up the whole city. "Is He here?" they called to one another.

"No, not in this one. Let's try that one over there!"

"Nope. No baby in here."

"Hey, guys! Come over here! I think I've found Him!"

The shepherds followed their friend's voice to the manger. Sure enough, there was a young couple there. And lying in the manger, wrapped in swaddling clothes, was a newborn baby. . .just like the angel said.

Dear Father, thank You for Jesus.

There's a Song in the Air

In the light of that star
Lie the ages impearled;
And that song from afar
Has swept over the world.
Every hearth is aflame,
And the beautiful sing
In the homes of the nations
That Jesus is King!

We rejoice in the light,
And we echo the song
That comes down through the night
From the heavenly throng.
Ay! We should to the lovely
Evangel they bring,
And we greet in His cradle
Our Savior and King!

JOSIAH HOLLAND

Feeding
the Birds

Consider the ravens: for they ther sow nor reap; which neither have storehouse nor barn; and God feedeth them: how much more are ye better than the fowls?

LUKE 12:24

"Tweet, tweet!" The birds chirp merrily in the trees. They are singing their praises to God. Although they don't have permanent houses, although they don't even have a place to keep their food, God always makes sure they have enough to eat. He takes care of them because He loves them.

On the night Jesus was born, there were animals nearby. They were cared for by their owners, tucked safely into a warm stable. Those owners must have loved their animals. God loves the animals, and He wants us to help Him take care of all of His creatures.

Just as the birds sing praises to God, who takes care of them, the animals in the stable that night may have praised Him for sending the newborn King to be born in their barn.

"Moo," called the cow.

"Baaa," cried the sheep.

"Oink, oink," said the pig.

God loves the animals and cares for them, and He loves us even more. He wants to take care of us. He wants us to trust Him for everything that we need, just as the animals do.

Dear Father, thank You for loving the animals. Please help me to love and care for my animals the way You want me to. Help me to trust You for everything that I need, just as the animals do.

GOOD CHRISTIAN MEN, REJOICE!

Good Christian men, rejoice
With heart and soul, and voice;
Give ye heed to what we say:
News! News! Jesus Christ is born today;
Ox and cow before Him bow;
And He is in the manger now.
Christ is born today! Christ is born today!

Good Christian men, rejoice,
With heart and soul and voice;
Now ye hear of endless bliss:
Joy! Joy! Jesus Christ was born for this!
He has opened the heavenly door,
And man is blest forevermore.
Christ was born for this!
Christ was born for this!

HEINRICH SUSO

TRANSLATED BY JOHN MASON NEALE

What Is Christmas?

*And the child grew, and waxed strong
in spirit, filled with wisdom:
and the grace of God was upon him.*

Luke 2:40

Christmas Day, December 25, is when the whole world celebrates Jesus' birthday. The celebration is not just one day long. People spend several weeks getting ready and celebrating with their family and friends. They read the Bible story that tells about Jesus' birth, and they go to church to learn more about Christmas. People decorate for Jesus' birthday, and they sing Christmas carols about Him.

Christmas reminds us of Baby Jesus in the manger, angels, shepherds, the star, and the wise men. It is a time to share gifts and treats and to enjoy little surprises. The closer it gets to Christmas, the more exited people become. They have waited all year for Christmas, as the people of long ago waited for Jesus to be born.

God wants people to always remember that Christmas is about Jesus' birthday. It is a time to celebrate Jesus' coming into the world, and it is a time to thank God for giving us Jesus—His most wonderful gift.

Dear Father, thank You for teaching me that Jesus is the only reason that we celebrate Christmas. On Christmas Day I will remember to say, "Happy Birthday, Jesus!"

LITTLE CHILDREN
CAN YOU SAY?

Little children can you say
Why you're glad on Christmas day;
Little children can you tell
Why you hear the sweet church bell;
Can you tell me who was born
Early on the Christmas morn?

This is the birthday of our King,
And we our little offering bring—
This is our Savior's holiday,
And therefore we are glad of this day;
We'll sing and pray and read His Word,
And keep the birthday of our Lord.

UNKNOWN

Angels Everywhere!

And suddenly there was with the angel a multitude of the heavenly host praising God, and saying, Glory to God in the highest, and on earth peace, good will toward men.

Luke 2:13-14

The angel sent the shepherds to Bethlehem. He even gave them a sign to look for, so they'd know they had found God's Son. But before the shepherds could even stand up, the sky filled with angels—more angels than they could count!

These angels weren't talking, though. They were singing! It was the most beautiful music the world had ever heard. Their music filled the skies with praises to God for sending His Son to earth.

Glory to God!" they sang. "Glory to God in the highest, and on earth peace!"

They knew that Jesus would provide the way for people to have peace with God. Jesus would make it possible for people to have their sins forgiven.

"Peace to men on whom His favor rests," the angels continued. They knew that the only reason God would send His Son to earth was because He loved people so much. God knew that the only way people could have peace was through Jesus Christ.

They sang and sang. We should sing, too, and praise Him every day for loving us.

Dear Father, thank You for loving us so much that You sent Jesus. Thank You for giving me peace. Help me to remember to sing songs to You, out loud and in my heart.

HARK! THE HERALD ANGELS SING

Hark! the herald angels sing,
"Glory to the newborn King;
Peace on earth, and mercy mild;
God and sinners reconciled."

Joyful, all ye nations rise,
Join the triumph of the skies;
With angelic hosts proclaim,
"Christ is born in Bethlehem."

CHARLES WESLEY

Good news!

And he said unto them, Go ye into all the world, and preach the gospel to every creature.

MARK 16:15

Sometimes the story of Jesus is called the Good News. On that very first Christmas, God sent His own Son, Jesus, into the world to save people and make a way for them to get to heaven. God wants everyone to spread that Good News so the whole world will know.

The shepherds were the first to share it. After they saw Baby Jesus, they told everyone they met. They told about the angel coming to them in the fields saying, "Do not be afraid! I have come to give you Good News. A baby was born tonight in Bethlehem. He is the One God promised would come to save the world." And those people the shepherds told shared the Good News with others, and the Good News kept going. . .and going. . .and going. . .and it is still being shared today.

You can help tell the world about Jesus. Tell your friends and family. Ask them to share the Good News, too: Jesus came to save the world and to show God's people the way to heaven!

Dear Father, teach me more about Jesus so I can tell all about Him. I want to share the Good News with everyone.

GO, TELL IT ON THE MOUNTAIN

Chorus:
Go, tell it on the mountain,
Over the hills and everywhere.
Go, tell it on the mountain,
That Jesus Christ is born.

Down in a lowly manger
The humble Christ was born
And God sent us salvation
That blessèd Christmas morn.

JOHN WESLEY WORK JR.
BASED ON AN AFRICAN-AMERICAN SPIRITUAL

Spreading
the Word

And when they had seen it, they made known abroad the saying which was told them concerning this child.

LUKE 2:17

The shepherds couldn't believe their eyes. They had searched and searched, and they'd found God's Son lying in a manger, just as the angel had said they would. This was the One they had heard stories about. This was the One they had waited their whole lives for. This was the One their parents and grandparents and great-grandparents had waited for.

After spending a few minutes looking at the baby, they knew they couldn't keep this news to themselves. "Let's go tell everyone," they whispered.

With a respectful bow, they slipped out of the stable. "Thank you for letting us see your baby," they whispered to Mary and Joseph as they left.

As soon as they were outside, they began to walk quickly. Then they began to run. "God's Son is here!" they shouted. "The One we've waited for has been born tonight, right here in Bethlehem! God has kept His promise. The Messiah has come at last!"

People may have stirred from their sleep. "Who is that, waking us up in the middle of the night?" they may have asked.

Some of them arose and went to see for themselves. Others may have pulled the covers over their heads and gone back to sleep. But no matter their response, the shepherds continued to tell everyone they met the good news: Jesus had arrived!

Dear Father, I want to be like the shepherds, telling everyone I know about Jesus.

BRING A TORCH, JEANETTE ISABELLA

Bring a torch, Jeanette, Isabella
Bring a torch, come swiftly and run
Christ is born, tell the folk of the
village Jesus is sleeping in His cradle
Ah, ah, beautiful is the Mother
Ah, ah, beautiful is her Son

Hasten now, good folk of the village
Hasten now, the Christ Child to see
You will find Him asleep in the manger
Quietly come and whisper softly
Hush, hush, peacefully now
He slumbers Hush, hush,
peacefully now He sleeps

TRADITIONAL FRENCH CAROL

Peace on Earth

*The wolf also shall dwell with the lamb,
and the leopard shall lie down with
the kid; and the calf and the young
lion and the fatling together;
and a little child shall lead them.*

Isaiah 11:6

Christmas is a happy time, and it is a peaceful time. Peaceful means "quiet" and "gentle." God wants everyone to be at peace with one another. He wants everyone to get along. One reason God sent Jesus to earth was to bring peace to the world. Someday, all people on earth will live peacefully together, and that will be because of Jesus. Even animals that do not get along will live together peacefully.

Animals were there the night Jesus was born. Animals might have been the first to see Baby Jesus. Some people think that Mary rode to Bethlehem on a donkey. So, a donkey might have been there. And Jesus was born in a place where animals stayed. His bed was their feeding box. Maybe cows and goats were there. The shepherds might have brought their sheep. Do you think the animals got along peacefully with one another?

How can you bring peace to your house?

Dear Father, please help me to get along with my family and friends. I think it feels good to be peaceful. I want everybody on earth to get along.

THE FRIENDLY BEASTS

Jesus our brother, kind and good
Was humbly born in a stable rude
And the friendly beasts
around Him stood,
Jesus our brother, kind and good.

"I," said the cow all white and red
"I gave Him my manger for His bed;
I gave him my hay to pillow his head."
"I," said the cow all white and red.

Thus every beast by some good spell,
In the stable dark was glad to tell
Of the gift he gave Immanuel,
The gift he gave Immanuel.

Traditional English Carol

Mary's Heart

And all they that heard it wondered at those things which were told them by the shepherds. But Mary kept all these things, and pondered them in her heart.

"Shhhhh. . ." Mary whispered. "Don't wake the baby." All evening, she had watched a steady stream of visitors file in and out of the stable. It had started with the shepherds. Then, they had told everyone they saw about her new baby. It didn't matter that it was the middle of the night. People were showing up in their night clothes just to get a look at Jesus.

Mary knew that Jesus was special. The angel had told her that He was God's Son. But she still didn't know all that would happen in Jesus' life. She wanted to remember every detail of this night. . .the night she gave birth to the promised Savior.

In many ways, Mary wasn't any different from other mothers. Every mother knows that her baby is special and wants to remember every detail about the day her baby was born. Throughout her baby's life, the mother thinks back on that special time when her child was small.

Later, Jesus went through some very hard things. People were mean to him. They even killed him. When those things happened, Mary was very sad. Remembering the sweet things about Jesus' birth and his childhood helped her to feel better.

Even though life was hard, she was always glad that God had chosen her to be Jesus' mother.

Dear Father, please help me to remember all the good things about my life. Help me to think about those things when I am sad.

SEE, AMID THE WINTER'S SNOW

Sacred Infant, all divine,
What a tender love was Thine,
Thus to come from highest bliss
Down to such a world as this.

Teach, O teach us, Holy Child,
By Thy face so meek and mild,
Teach us to resemble Thee,
In Thy sweet humility.

EDWARD CASWELL AND SIR JOHN GOSS

Light of
the World

As long as I am in the world,
I am the light of the world.

John 9:5

Light was an important part of that first Christmas long ago. On the night Jesus was born, the angels came to the shepherds in a great, bright light, and Jesus' star lit up the sky to show the way to Bethlehem.

Today at Christmas time, people use light to celebrate Jesus' birthday. They decorate their houses with Christmas lights and put lights on Christmas trees. Candlelight is a part of Christmas, too. Candles light up churches, and some people light candles in their houses.

Another name for Jesus is "the Light of the world." That is because when He grew up, Jesus told people, "I am the light of the world" (John 8:12). He meant that He would help all the people in the world see the way to heaven. Jesus' love is like a bright, warm light. Believing that He came to show the way to heaven is like seeing Him shine a dazzling light on a dark path.

Whenever you see Christmas lights, think about Jesus. Remember the angels appearing to the shepherds in a burst of white light, and remember Jesus' star shining brightly in the sky.

Dear Jesus, from now on when I see Christmas lights, I will think of You and remember Your birthday. Thank You for being the Light of the world.

THIS LITTLE LIGHT O' MINE

This little light o' mine,
I'm goin' let it shine,
This little light o' mine,
I'm goin' let it shine,
This little light o' mine,
I'm goin' let it shine,
Let it shine, let it shine, let it shine.

Everywhere I go, I'm goin' let it shine,

Everywhere I go, I'm goin' let it shine,

Everywhere I go, I'm goin' let it shine,

Let it shine, let it shine, let it shine.

HARRY DIXON LOES

Anna

[Anna] was a widow of about fourscore and four years, which departed not from the temple, but served God with fastings and prayers night and day. And she coming in that instant gave thanks likewise unto the Lord, and spake of him to all them that looked for redemption in Jerusalem.

Luke 2:37–38

Anna was very old. She never had any children of her own, and her husband had died a long time ago. She spent most of her life at the temple, praising God and helping out in any way she could.

She loved God very much, and she wanted to serve Him. She knew one of the best ways to serve God was to stay at the temple. That way, she would be ready if somebody there needed something.

Some people might have grown tired of serving God, but not Anna. She never said, "I think I'll stay home today. I'd rather visit with my neighbors, or sew myself a new dress." She knew she was supposed to be at the temple, serving God. Because she obeyed God, she was at the temple when Mary and Joseph arrived with baby Jesus. She got to hold God's Son, and be among the first to announce His arrival to the world.

Like Anna, we need to serve God and obey Him every day. That way, we will always be where we are supposed to be. We never know when God may choose to show up and bless us.

Dear Father, I want to serve You like Anna did. I love You.

In the Bleak Midwinter

Angels and archangels
May have gathered there,
Cherubim and seraphim
Thronged the air;
But his mother only,
In her maiden bliss,
Worshipped the Beloved
With a kiss.

What can I give him,
Poor as I am?
If I were a shepherd
I would bring a lamb,
If I were a wise man
I would do my part,
Yet what I can I give Him —
Give my heart.

CHRISTINA ROSSETTI

Christmas Dinner

But when thou makest a feast,
call the poor, the maimed, the lame,
the blind: and thou shalt be blessed;
for they cannot recompense thee:
for thou shalt be recompensed
at the resurrection of the just.

LUKE 14:13–14

In Jesus' time, people celebrated special days with a feast—a big dinner. People do the same today, especially on holidays like Christmas. People remember Jesus' birthday with Christmas dinner. Turkey, ham, potatoes, vegetables, pies, cakes: There is so much yummy food to eat and plenty left over to share.

Jesus reminded people to share their feast with others, especially those who do not have enough. One way that people share their food is by giving some to food banks. Community helpers collect food to give to the hungry. Jesus said that when people give something away, they should expect nothing in return. Giving to help someone makes you feel good. And when Jesus sees you giving, that makes Him feel good, too.

Talk with your family about giving. Why is it important to share what you have with those who do not have enough? How can you help the hungry?

Dear Father, I want everyone to have a happy time celebrating Jesus' birthday. Remind me to share what I have and to give to those who do not have enough.

Good King Wenceslas

Good King Wenceslas looked out
on the Feast of Stephen,
When the snow lay round about,
deep and crisp and even.
Brightly shone the moon that night,
though the frost was cruel,
When a poor man came in sight,
gath'ring winter fuel.

"Hither, page, and stand by me,
if you know it, telling,
Yonder peasant, who is he?
Where and what his dwelling?"
"Sire, he lives a good league hence,
underneath the mountain,
Right against the forest fence,
by Saint Agnes' fountain."

"Bring me food and bring me wine,
bring me pine logs hither,
You and I will see him dine,
when we bear them thither."
Page and monarch, forth they went,
forth they went together,
Through the cold wind's wild lament
and the bitter weather.

JOHN M. NEALE

The Wise Men

Now when Jesus was born in Bethlehem
of Judaea in the days of Herod the king,
behold, there came wise men from the
east to Jerusalem, saying, Where is he
that is born King of the Jews? for we
have seen his star in the east,
and are come to worship him.

MATTHEW 2:1–2

"Look at that star!" The man pointed, and his friends looked at the sky. The man and his friends were very smart. They had spent years studying the stars. They believed they could learn things about God by watching His creation.

"Do you think that's the one?" asked another man. "Could that be the star that will lead us to God's Son?"

"Let's go find out," replied the first man. The wise men packed up their belongings and left right away. They didn't care how long it took them. They were ready to travel as far as they needed to, so they could see Jesus. After a long time, they found Jesus and his parents. They knew they were in the presence of God's Son.

The wise men looked for Jesus, and they knew they would find Him. We can look for Jesus, too. Oh, we may not see Him in person. Still, we can look for ways that He shows His love to us. We can look for ways to show His love to other people, for when we show His love, Jesus is there.

Dear Father, thank You for sending
the wise men to Jesus. I want to be wise, too.
I want to spend each day seeking Your
love and Your plan for my life.

We Three Kings of Orient Are

Glorious now behold him arise

King and God and Sacrifice

Alleluia, Alleluia

Earth to heav'n replies

Chorus:

O star of wonder, star of night

Star with royal beauty bright,

Westward leading, still proceeding,

Guide us to thy perfect light.

JOHN H. HOPKINS

Family Time

[I] will be a Father unto you,
and ye shall be my sons and daughters,
saith the Lord Almighty.

2 CORINTHIANS 6:18

Christmas is a special time for families. Moms, dads, sons, daughters, sisters, brothers, aunts, uncles, cousins, grandparents—they all get together to celebrate Jesus' birthday!

Families around the world celebrate in different ways. In South Africa, Christmas comes in summertime. Instead of a big Christmas dinner, families get together for a barbeque lunch. In Mexico, people walk down the streets singing Christmas songs as they remember Mary and Joseph looking for a place to stay in Bethlehem. In Germany, children write letters to Baby Jesus and leave them on windowsills. All over the world going to church is an important part of a family Christmas.

Families wish each other "Merry Christmas" in different ways. In France they say, "Joyeux Noel." In Mexico: "Feliz Navidad." And in Hawaii: "Mele Kalikimaka."

Families come in many sizes. Some are big. Some are small. But all families who believe that Jesus came to save the world are part of God's one big family. He is the heavenly Father, and they are His children.

Does your family have a special way to celebrate Christmas?

Dear Father, thank You for my family.
And thank You for being my heavenly Father.
I feel special knowing that I belong to You.

DECK THE HALL

Deck the hall with boughs of holly,
Fa la la la la, la la la la,
'Tis the season to be jolly,
Fa la la la la, la la la la.
Don we now our gay apparel,
Fa-la-la-la-la, la-la-la-la,
Troll the ancient Christmas carol,
Fa la la la la, la la la la.

Fast away the old year passes,

Fa-la-la-la-la, la-la-la-la,

Hail the new, ye lads and lasses,

Fa-la-la-la-la, la-la-la-la

Sing we joyous all together,

Fa-la-la-la-la, la-la-la-la,

Heedless of the wind and weather,

Fa-la-la-la-la, la-la-la-la.

OLD WELSH CAROL

King Herod

When Herod the king had heard
these things, he was troubled,
and all Jerusalem with him.

MATTHEW 2:3

The wise men traveled a long time looking for Jesus. They had to stop to rest and for food and water. When they stopped, they talked to the people who lived in that place. "We're looking for the newborn king," they said excitedly.

One night, they stopped in King Herod's town. When Herod heard the men were looking for the king of the Jews, he was concerned. *I'm the king,* he thought. *Who is this baby they are looking for?* He became worried that someone was trying to take his job from him.

Herod wanted to find out who this baby was. He wanted to make the baby and his family go away, so they wouldn't try to take his job. He didn't understand that Jesus' kingdom wasn't here on earth.

Herod pretended to be interested in baby Jesus. He told the men, "When you find the baby, come back and tell me where He is, so I can send him a present. I want to worship Him, too."

But Herod didn't really want to send a gift. He didn't really want to worship Jesus. He wanted to kill Him.

If Herod had only taken time to find out more about this baby, he would have known that Jesus didn't come to be an earthly king. He came to be the king of our hearts.

Dear Father, thank You for sending
Jesus to be the King of my heart.
I want to worship You with my life.

THE BIRTHDAY OF A KING

In the little village of Bethlehem,
There lay a Child one day;
And the sky was bright with a holy light
O'er the place where Jesus lay.

Alleluia! O how the angels sang!

Alleluia! How it rang!

And the sky was

bright with a holy light

'Twas the birthday of a King.

WILLIAM H. NEIDLINGER

Friends!

Ye are my friends,
if ye do whatsoever I command you.

Friends have fun celebrating Christmas together. There are so many things to do. Friends bake Christmas cookies and make a birthday cake for Jesus. They sing Christmas carols and make little gifts and surprises. Friends act in Christmas plays at church, and they hear about Jesus' birthday in Sunday school. They decorate Christmas trees together and play games and wish each other a "Merry Christmas!"

Jesus loved spending time with His friends. He liked visiting two sisters and a brother named Mary, Martha, and Lazarus. And Jesus had twelve helper-friends called *disciples*. They were Peter, Andrew, James and James (two Jameses!), John, Philip, Bartholomew, Matthew, Thomas, Simon, Thaddeus, and Judas Iscariot. Do you have any friends with those names?

Jesus made friends everywhere He went, and He is your friend, too! Jesus is your best friend because He knows you better than anyone else. He loves you just the way you are, and He always has time for you. Jesus helps you and watches over you day and night.

What do you and your friends do together to celebrate His birthday?

Dear Jesus, You are my best friend.
I like it that You love me just as I am and that
You always have time for me. I can tell You
anything and know that You will hear me.

JINGLE BELLS

Dashing thro' the snow,
In a one horse open sleigh,
O'er the hills we go,
Laughing all the way;
Bells on bob tail ring,
Making spirits bright,
Oh what sport to ride and sing
A sleighing song to night.

Chorus:

Jingle bells, jingle bells,

Jingle all the way;

Oh! what joy it is to ride

In a one horse open sleigh.

Jingle bells, jingle bells,

Jingle all the way

Oh! what joy it is to ride

In a one horse open sleigh.

JAMES LORD PIERPONT

Following the Star

When they had heard the king,
they departed; and, lo, the star,
which they saw in the east, went before
them, till it came and stood over where the
young child was. When they saw the star,
they rejoiced with exceeding great joy.

MATTHEW 2:9–10

"There it is. Let's go that way!" one of the wise men called to his friends. "I think we're getting closer."

The wise men traveled for a long time. Night after night, month after month, for more than two years they followed that star! The star kept moving, guiding them to where they needed to be. At times, they probably grew tired. They may have wondered if they would ever reach their destination. Maybe they even thought about turning around and going home.

But they kept going. They didn't give up. Finally, the star stopped over the house where Jesus lived with his parents. They couldn't believe their eyes! Was their journey finally coming to an end?

As the wise men approached the house, they were filled with joy. At last, they would see the One they had searched for! At last, they would meet God's Son, Jesus. They knew this was a very special day, indeed.

The wise men followed the star. They went where God led them, and He gave them joy. When we follow God, He helps us to feel joyful, too.

Dear Father, I'm glad the wise men
followed where You led them.
I want to follow You, too.

THE FIRST NOEL

The first Noel the angel did say
Was to certain poor shepherds
in fields as they lay;
In fields where they lay
keeping their sheep,
On a cold winter's night
that was so deep.

And by the light
of that same Star,
Three wise men came
from country far;
To seek for a King
was their intent,
And to follow the Star
wherever it went.

OLD ENGLISH CAROL

Christmas Wishes

*A new commandment I give unto you,
that ye love one another; as I have
loved you, that ye also love one another.*

John 13:34

Some people wish for big things that are new and special. Some wish for everyday things like a warm house, clean clothes, and plenty of food to eat. Some wish for friends.

All year, and especially at Christmas, you can help people get what they wish for by being God's helper.

Jesus loved everybody, and when He grew up He helped many people. When they were sick, Jesus helped them to be well again. When they were hungry, He found ways to feed them. But most of all, Jesus taught people to love and help one another.

You can help at Christmastime by thinking about what people need and then finding ways to make their wishes come true. Maybe your Sunday school class can visit lonely people in nursing homes or help older people in your church with yard work or snow shoveling.

Talk with your family about ways that you can help others at Christmas. See if you can make someone's wishes come true.

Dear Father, I want to help people
not just at Christmas but every day.
Help me to see what they need.
Then give me ideas for ways I can help.

We Wish You a Merry Christmas

We wish you a merry Christmas,
We wish you a merry Christmas,
We wish you a merry Christmas,
And a happy New Year!

Chorus:

Good tidings we bring
for you and your kin;
We wish you a merry Christmas
and a happy New Year!

TRADITIONAL ENGLISH CAROL

Gifts for
Baby Jesus

And when they were come into the house,
they saw the young child with Mary his
mother, and fell down, and worshipped
him: and when they had opened their
treasures, they presented unto him gifts;
gold, and frankincense and myrrh.

MATTHEW 2:11

The wise men could hardly believe their eyes! They had traveled for so long, and at times they had wondered if they would ever reach the new king. But there in front of them was a house. The star they had followed stood still, directly over that house. They knocked on the door, and Mary answered. "May I help you?" she asked.

"We're here to see God's Son. Is He here?"

"Yes, He is." She invited them in. Maybe she offered them something to eat or drink. But no matter how tired and thirsty the men were, they probably had only one thing on their minds. They wanted to see God's Son!

Jesus was about two years old. Perhaps He was eating His lunch, or building with some blocks. The men came right in and knelt down in front of Jesus.

They gave Him gifts, too. The gifts were expensive gifts, suitable for a king. Jesus was too young to understand how nice the gifts were. Mary thanked them and put the gifts away, for when Jesus was older.

We can give Jesus gifts, too. Oh, we may not have fancy gifts like the wise men gave. But the thing Jesus wants most is our hearts. When we love Him with our whole hearts, we give Him the most precious gift of all.

Dear Father, I love You. Please help me
to love you more each day,
with my whole heart.

THE FIRST NOEL

This Star drew nigh to the northwest,
O'er Bethlehem it took its rest,
And there it did both stop and stay,
Right over the place where Jesus lay.

Then entered in those wise men three,

Full rev'rently upon their knee,

And offered there in His presence,

Their gold, and myrrh,

and frankincense.

OLD ENGLISH CAROL

Christmas Eve

And one cried unto another, and said,
Holy, holy, holy, is the Lord of hosts:
the whole earth is full of his glory.

Isaiah 6:3

Christmas Eve is a holy night. That means it is a night to spend thinking about God. People wait all year for Christmas Eve. They wait like those people from long ago waited for God to keep His promise. But people today know that God *did* keep His promise! He sent Jesus to save the world, and Christmas Eve is one special night to remember and celebrate that promise. It is a night to think about Mary and Joseph going to Bethlehem, Jesus in the manger, angels, shepherds, and wise men. It is a night for church and candlelight and thanking God for His wonderful gifts.

People celebrate Christmas with lights, trees, cookies, songs, and presents, but Jesus is much more important than those things. He is the one true reason that Christmas is celebrated all around the world. If God had not kept His promise to send Jesus, there would be no Christmas. It would be just like any other day.

Ask someone to read aloud the Christmas story in the Bible: Luke 2:1–20.

Dear Father, I love celebrating Jesus' birthday! Thank You for sending Him to earth. And thank You for teaching me about Him and the real meaning of Christmas.

O Holy Night

O holy night,
the stars are brightly shining,
It is the night of
the dear Savior's birth;
Long lay the world in sin
and error pining,
Till he appeared and the
soul felt its worth.
A thrill of hope the
weary world rejoices,
For yonder breaks a new
and glorious morn.

Chorus:
Fall on your knees!
Oh, hear the angel voices!
O night divine!
O night when Christ was born.
O night, O holy night,
O night divine.

PLACIDE CAPPEAU

The Greatest Gift

*For God so loved the world, that he gave
his only begotten Son, that whosoever
believeth in him should not perish,
but have everlasting life.*

Christmas is a fun time, filled with surprises and brightly wrapped gifts. Everywhere we go, we see beautifully decorated wreaths and hear festive music. Christmas brings fun secrets and delicious food. For many people, Christmas is the most wonderful time of the year.

The colorful trees are pretty, but they aren't the reason we celebrate Christmas. The music is nice to listen to, but it's not the reason for Christmas either. The gifts are fun to open, but even they are not the reason we celebrate Christmas. The purpose of the season is not about the gifts we receive on Christmas morning. It's about the gift that God gave a long time ago.

Jesus is the reason we celebrate Christmas. The word *Christmas* actually comes from His name—Christ. We celebrate Christmas because God loved us so much that He sent His Son, Jesus, to live with us. Jesus lived His life for us, so we could see how to live. Then He gave His life for us, to take the punishment for our sins. No matter how great the new bicycles and the dolls and the games and the new puppies may seem, none of those gifts compares to the true gift of Christmas: Jesus Christ.

God gave us a gift, and we can give a gift back to Him. He loves us, and He wants us to love Him, too. When we choose to love Him with our whole hearts, we give Him the perfect gift.

Dear Father, thank You for giving the greatest gift of all time—Your Son.

O Little Town of Bethlehem

How silently, how silently
The wondrous Gift is giv'n!
So God imparts to human hearts
The blessings of His Heav'n.
No ear may hear His coming;
But in this world of sin,
Where meek souls will receive Him still,
The dear Christ enters in.

O holy Child of Bethlehem,
Descend to us, we pray;
Cast out our sin and enter in,
Be born in us today.
We hear the Christmas angels
The great glad tidings tell—
O come to us, abide with us,
Our Lord Emmanuel.

PHILLIPS BROOKS

Presents!

Every good gift and every perfect gift is from above, and cometh down from the Father of lights, with whom is no variableness, neither shadow of turning.

JAMES 1:17

Kids love presents! Grown-ups do, too. Christmas is a time for giving and getting presents. Wrapped packages under Christmas trees hold all kinds of surprises. What could be inside? Maybe a doll, a truck, a game, pajamas, or even underwear! Stockings hang stuffed with little gifts like candy, a toothbrush, a book, or crayons.

People give presents at Christmas to remember that the wise men brought gifts to Baby Jesus. The wise men brought expensive gifts fit for a king. But Christmas gifts do not have to be expensive. The best gifts might surprise you because they do not come in boxes wrapped in brightly colored paper.

Spending time together, making someone happy, being gentle and kind, sharing, and being patient—all of these are gifts of love, and love is the best gift of all.

The Bible says that God is love. Because God loved people so much, He gave them Jesus. And Jesus loved people so much that He made a way for them to live forever in heaven.

"Thank You, God, for Your gifts of love!"

Dear Father, thank You for Christmas presents, but most of all thank You for love.

THE TWELVE DAYS OF CHRISTMAS

On the twelfth day of Christmas,
My true love sent to me
Twelve lords a-leaping,
Eleven ladies dancing,
Ten pipers piping,
Nine drummers drumming,
Eight maids a-milking,

Seven swans a-swimming,

Six geese a-laying,

Five golden rings.

Four calling birds,

Three French hens,

Two turtle-doves and

A partridge in a pear tree.

TRADITIONAL ENGLISH CAROL

Feeding the Sheep

Lovest thou me? . . . Feed my sheep.

John 21:17

At Christmas, we think about Jesus, God's gift to us. We think about giving gifts to others, and we take extra effort to make those gifts special. We save our money, we wrap the gifts in shiny paper, and we wait with excitement for those gifts to be opened.

But Jesus wants us to be gift-givers every single day. He wants us to share the gift of His love with everyone we meet. After all, people need to know that He loves them all the time, not just at Christmastime! They need His love each day of their lives.

In a way, Jesus wants us to be like the shepherds in the Christmas story. The people we meet are like the sheep. He wants us to care for them and feed them with His love. When we do that, we give them the greatest gift. We also give Jesus a gift, too, as we do what He asks us to do.

Dear Father, I love You, and I want to feed Your sheep. Help me to share Your love with everyone I meet, all year long.

O Holy Night

Truly He taught us
to love one another,
His law is love and
His gospel is peace.
Long live His truth,
and may it last forever,
For in His name all
discordant noise shall cease.

Sweet hymns of joy
in grateful chorus raise we,
With all our hearts
we praise His holy name.
Christ is the Lord!
Then ever, ever praise we,
His power and glory
ever more proclaim!
His power and glory
ever more proclaim!

Traditional French Carol

The Best Gift of All

Evening, and morning, and at noon,
will I pray, and cry aloud:
and he shall hear my voice.

PSALM 55:17

Now you know all about Christmas. You know that God loves His people. He made a promise, and He kept it. He sent His Son, Jesus, into the world as a baby, and everything that God planned happened. Jesus grew up, and He made a way for people to get to heaven some day—but that is another story for another time.

Christmas is Jesus' birthday. It is a time to have fun and celebrate. But, even more, it is a time to remember and thank God for Jesus.

Praying is talking to God. You can talk with Him all the time because God loves hearing your prayers. You can pray to tell God what is going on in your life. You can ask Him for something for yourself or for others. And you can tell Him "thank You."

Thank God for His blessings. Thank Him for your family and friends. Thank Him for loving you and watching over you. And especially thank God for giving you the best Christmas present of all—Jesus!

Tonight, make up your own bedtime prayer. Tell God some of the things you have learned about Christmas.

Here We Come A-Caroling (reprise)

God bless the Master of this house,
Likewise the Mistress too
And all the little children,
That round the table go.

Chorus:
Love and joy come to you,
And to your carol, too,
And God bless you and send you a
happy New Year,
And God send you a
happy New Year.

TRADITIONAL ENGLISH CAROL

SCRIPTURE INDEX

Luke

ABOUT THE AUTHORS

Renae Brumbaugh lives in Texas with her two noisy children and two dogs. She's authored four books in Barbour's Camp Club Girls series, *Morning Coffee with James* (Chalice Press), and has contributed to several anthologies. Her humor column and articles have appeared in publications across the country.

Jean Fischer's writing career began in the 1980s when she worked as an editor for a leading children's book publisher. Today, she writes full time. Jean has written many Christian books for adults and children. Home is Racine, Wisconsin, where she enjoys the beauty of Lake Michigan, woodland wildlife, and her backyard gardens.